Dear Revathi,

It was a double treat for me to work with you in two grade levels! You've made so much progress as a student!

You are creative and talented in so many areas — work hard and you'll go far!

You're special to me — I'll miss you! Keep in touch.

Best wishes for Middle School!

Love,
Jane Erera
grade 5
June 17, 1994

FREEDOM DOCUMENTS

Troll Associates

FREEDOM DOCUMENTS

by Francene Sabin

Illustrated by Bob Dole

Troll Associates

Library of Congress Cataloging in Publication Data

Sabin, Francene.
  Freedom documents.

  Summary: A brief description of the Declaration
of Independence and the Constitution, the documents
on which the laws of our country are based.
    1. United States. Declaration of Independence—
Juvenile literature.   2. United States. Constitution—
Juvenile literature.   3. United States—Constitutional
history—Juvenile literature.   [1. United States.
Declaration of Independence.   2. United States.
Constitution]   I. Dole, Bob, ill.   II. Title.
E221.S15   1985   973.3'13   84-8596
ISBN 0-8167-0238-1 (lib. bdg.)
ISBN 0-8167-0239-X (pbk.)

Long before the start of the American Revolution, the colonists in the New World felt mistreated by the British government. They did not have the representation in Parliament that was enjoyed by British subjects in England. They were heavily taxed. Worst of all, the rights guaranteed by British law were denied to the colonists.

7

The colonists protested against this unfairness in many ways. They refused to pay unjust taxes. They sent delegations to plead their case in England. They dumped British tea into Boston Harbor. They published essays and made speeches to publicize their cause.

In colony after colony, local groups took up arms. But most colonists still wanted peace. They wanted to remain a part of Great Britain.

It soon became clear, however, that Great Britain would never give in to the demands of the American Colonies. That left the Colonies little choice but to declare the independence toward which they were already moving.

In fact, an American army, authorized by the Continental Congress and led by George Washington, was already fighting against British troops. And many colonists were openly rebelling against the Crown.

In June 1776, a resolution was proposed to the Congress by Richard Henry Lee, a delegate from Virginia. It said, "That these United Colonies are, and of right ought to be, free and independent States, that they are absolved from all allegiance to the British Crown, and that all political connection between them and the State of Great Britain is, and ought to be, totally dissolved."

After heated debate, the resolution was passed unanimously, and a committee of five was appointed to draw up a Declaration of Independence. The committee members were Benjamin Franklin of Pennsylvania, John Adams of Massachusetts, Robert Livingston of New York, Roger Sherman of Connecticut, and Thomas Jefferson of Virginia.

Because Jefferson was considered the best writer of the five, he was asked to draft the document. The result was a remarkable piece of work, which needed only a few changes before being adopted by Congress on July 2, 1776. It was signed two days later on July 4.

The Declaration of Independence can be divided into four parts. The first part, called the *Preamble*, says that when people decide to dissolve their political ties and become a separate nation, they should declare the reasons for their actions.

The second part of the Declaration is called *A Declaration of Rights.* It is a long section stating the philosophy of independence.

It begins with these words: "We hold these truths to be self-evident, that all men are created equal, that they are endowed by their Creator with certain unalienable rights, that among these are life, liberty, and the pursuit of happiness. That to secure these rights, governments are instituted among men, deriving their just powers from the consent of the governed."

The idea that all people are equal and have rights that no one may take away was not a new one in 1776. But it had never before been expressed so simply and so powerfully.

The third part of the Declaration is known as *A Bill of Indictment.* It consists of a list of charges against King George III of Great Britain.

Jefferson cleverly put the blame directly on King George for every ill the Colonies had suffered. Jefferson knew that the colonists would respond more favorably to criticism of King George than to criticism of the British nation, because many of the colonists still had close ties with the British.

14

The final section of the document is called *A Statement of Independence*, and it includes Richard Henry Lee's resolution. To make sure that everyone knew how determined the members of the Congress were, Jefferson ended with these words: "And for the support of this declaration... we mutually pledge to each other our lives, our fortunes, and our sacred honor."

When the Revolutionary War finally ended in American victory, the new states joined together in a confederation. A confederation is a body of loosely united, independent states.

Under the Articles of Confederation, the document that defined this system, the central government had almost no power at all. Each state printed its own money, raised its own army, and had almost every power enjoyed by an individual nation.

It soon became clear that confederation
was not working. The value of money
varied too much from one state to another.
With each state taxing the goods imported
from other states, trade became next-to-
impossible. The unity the Colonies had felt
during the war with England was rapidly
dissolving into chaos.

To remedy the situation, a convention was called in the spring of 1787, to revise the Articles of Confederation. A majority of the fifty-five delegates at the convention in Philadelphia's Independence Hall came to the conclusion that the country needed a new, strong constitution.

But the delegates disagreed with each other on many points. One state, Rhode Island, hadn't even sent a delegate to the convention. But the problems were overcome, one by one.

Each dispute was settled by compromise. For example, the larger states wanted representation in Congress to be based on population. This was called the Virginia Plan, because that state had proposed it.

The smaller states, however, wanted representation to be equal from each state. This was the New Jersey Plan, proposed by that state. The solution, proposed by Connecticut, came to be called the Great Compromise.

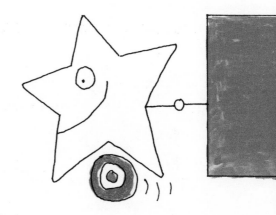

Under the Great Compromise, representation in the House of Representatives would be based on population, while representation in the Senate would be equal for all states.

Other compromises in the Constitution dealt with slavery, with the number of states needed to ratify, or approve, the Constitution, and with the rights of the states and of the people. At last, an acceptable Constitution was written and signed on September 17, 1787.

The Constitution of the United States is made up of a preamble, seven articles that describe the powers and workings of the federal government, and a number of amendments, or additions. The first ten amendments, known as the Bill of Rights, were also the results of compromise.

The Bill of Rights guarantees that the government will not take away or limit the natural rights of the people. These are the same rights of which Thomas Jefferson wrote in the Declaration of Independence.

The first amendment says that Congress may not make laws denying freedom of speech, of religion, of the press, of the right to assemble in peaceful groups, and of the right to petition the government to correct grievances.

Other amendments in the Bill of Rights protect people against unlawful arrests and seizure of property, and guarantee the right to *due process of law*, or fair treatment under the law.

Finally, the Bill of Rights says that rights not specifically described in the Constitution belong to the people; and that powers not given to the federal government or prohibited to the states belong to the states and the people.

With the Bill of Rights guaranteeing that the new government would not be a tyranny, as the British Crown had been, the Constitution took effect. And the American government, as it exists today, began to operate.

This government consists of three equal branches—the executive, the legislative, and the judicial. The executive branch, led by the President, *enforces* the laws of the United States. The legislative branch, which *makes* the laws, consists of the two Houses of

Congress. These are the Senate and the House of Representatives. The judicial branch *explains* the laws. It is made up of the Supreme Court of the United States and a number of lower federal courts.

The Supreme Court is the final authority on all laws passed by the federal government or by any of the fifty states. The Supreme Court can throw out any law which disagrees with the Constitution. That is because the Constitution is the law of the land.

The Constitution of the United States is not a perfect document. But its authors never expected to produce perfection. They knew that, even with good sense and wisdom, people would disagree. They also knew that time would bring changes and call for new amendments to the Constitution.

Proof that they were right is that there are now more than twenty-five amendments to the Constitution. These amendments provided for an income tax, extended voting to women, ended slavery, and gave civil rights to all people.

Other amendments dealt with the
succession to the presidency and changes in
voting and representation in the Houses of
Congress. A few of the amendments to the
Constitution have dealt with the technical
workings of government.

But most of the amendments have served to extend the "unalienable rights" described in the Declaration of Independence to people who had not yet received them. In this way, the Constitution continues to live and to grow, and to be a model for governments everywhere.